Anurag Rana

Net Neutrality. Developing Business Model and Evidence Based Net Neutrality Regulation

GRIN Publishing

Bibliographic information published by the German National Library:

The German National Library lists this publication in the National Bibliography; detailed bibliographic data are available on the Internet at http://dnb.dnb.de .

Imprint:

Copyright © 2014 GRIN Verlag GmbH
Print and binding: Books on Demand GmbH, Norderstedt Germany
ISBN: 978-3-656-66945-6

This book at GRIN:

http://www.grin.com/en/e-book/274066/net-neutrality-developing-business-model-and-evidence-based-net-neutrality

GRIN - Your knowledge has value

Since its foundation in 1998, GRIN has specialized in publishing academic texts by students, college teachers and other academics as e-book and printed book. The website www.grin.com is an ideal platform for presenting term papers, final papers, scientific essays, dissertations and specialist books.

Visit us on the internet:

http://www.grin.com/

http://www.facebook.com/grincom

http://www.twitter.com/grin_com

NETWORK NEUTRALITY:
Developing Business Model and Evidence Based net neutrality Regulation

Mr. ANURAG RANA

ABSTRACT

Over the past ten years, the debate over "network neutrality" has remained one of the central debates in Internet policy. Governments all over the world have been investigating whether legislative or regulatory action is needed to limit the ability of providers of Internet access services to interfere with the applications, content and services on their networks. Net neutrality' comprises two separate non-discrimination commitments. Backward-looking 'net neutrality lite' claims that Internet users should not be disadvantaged due to opaque and invidious practices by their current Internet Service Provider (ISP). Forward-looking 'positive net neutrality' is a principle whereby higher Quality of Service (QoS) for higher prices should be offered on fair, reasonable and non-discriminatory (FRAND) terms to all-comers. Neither extreme in the debate is an optimum solution. There is too much at stake to expect government to supplant the market in providing higher-speed connections, or for the market to continue to deliver without basic policy and regulatory backstops to ensure continued openness. Permitting content discrimination on the Internet will permit much more granular knowledge of what an ISP's customers are doing on the Internet. A co-regulatory regime will ensure oversight and remove the most obvious abuses by fixed and mobile ISPs. Beyond rules that forbid network providers from blocking applications, content and services, non-discrimination rules are a key component of any network neutrality regime.

This analytical study provides background on the debate over network neutrality, including the implications for business models going forward that have been attempted and that are currently in play. This article explains for a global policy audience what the regulatory and governance problems and potential solutions are for the issue referred to as 'network neutrality', unpacking its 'lite' and 'heavy' elements. Eschewing technical, economic or legalistic explanations previously tackled elsewhere, it explains that increasing Internet Service Provider (ISP) control over content risks not just differentiated pricing and speed on the Internet. It explains that a co-regulatory regime may ensure regulatory oversight and remove obvious abuses by fixed and mobile ISPs, without preventing innovation, while guarding against government abuse of the censorship opportunities provided by new technologies.

Keywords: Net Neutrality, Internet Provider, Non-Discrimination, QoS.

I INTRODUCTION

What constitutes network neutrality? Several definitions are in current use:

- The ability of all Internet users to access the content or applications of their choice.
- Assurance that all traffic on the Internet is treated equally, whatever its source, content or destination.
- Absence of *unreasonable discrimination* on the part of network operators in transmitting Internet traffic[4].

These definitional differences are not a mere matter of semantics. They differ in (1) the degree of focus on access, versus the *quality* of access, versus the *price* of access to content and applications; and (2) whether one should be concerned with all forms of differentiation, or only with those that are anticompetitive, discriminatory, or otherwise unreasonable. It is worth noting at this point that the concern here is not only with traditional text and audiovisual content, but also with services such as search engines (such as Yahoo, Google, and Bing) and voice over IP (such as Skype and Viber). The use of various forms of *quality differentiation* for Internet traffic has been routine for decades. Departures from network neutrality (i.e. unreasonable discrimination) could raise a number of quite distinct potential issues of societal welfare, among them:

Anticompetitive behavior: Is there a risk that a network operator with significant market power (SMP) might project its market power into upstream or downstream market segments that would otherwise be competitive?

Innovation: Might a network operator (especially a vertically integrated network operator that possesses some form of market power) act as a gatekeeper, inhibiting the ability of content providers or application service providers with which it competes from offering new, innovative products or services?

Freedom of expression: Might a network operator interfere with the ability of its customers to express views with which the network operator disagrees?

Consumer awareness: Do consumers understand the service that is being offered to them, and are they receiving the service that has been committed?

Privacy: To the extent that a network operator treats some Internet traffic differently from other traffic, does this necessarily imply that the network operator is delving more deeply than it should into the user's personal affairs (e.g. by means of *Deep Packet Inspection [DPI]*)?

II DEVELOPING BUSINESS MODELS

An Emergence of the two-lane model

Initially, the net neutrality discussions focused on the different treatment of traffic flows in the public Internet. The public Internet is a global system of interconnected networks that use the IP protocol to transport data between the connected end points. The adjective "public" in public internet emphasis that ends users can access all information and applications on the global Internet from their own end point. This information and the applications are offered, either for free or in exchange for payment, by content providers that are connected to an Internet end point themselves as well. The role of the public Internet is essentially that of a transport network that connects users and applications providers across the globe. In principle, the Internet can support all IP-based services and applications by transporting IP traffic between application or content providers and users worldwide. Broadband ISPs play an important role in the public Internet, as they provide the Internet Access Service: the part of the Internet transport chain between the home network or mobile terminal of the user and the larger ISPs that collectively comprise the Internet core. In general, the Internet access service is a best-effort service, e.g., there are no guarantees that IP packets sent over the network reach their destination end point within a certain time. This type of best-effort Internet access services matches the best-effort characteristics of the Internet core.

Providers of Internet Access Services increasingly provide other IP-based services in parallel with the Internet access service over same infrastructure. Two well-known examples here are IPTV and IP telephony services provided by a range of European ISPs over their DSL, cable and fiber access networks. Although these services are delivered over the same network infrastructure as the Internet Access Service, they can in a number of respects be distinct from the Internet Access Service. Often, they are offered as "managed services". Other terms that are used are "managed or specialized services"[3] or "additional, differentiated online services". The adjective "managed" can be slightly misleading here, as it does not provide a clear demarcation between these newer forms and the traditional public Internet access service. Although the Internet access service and the Internet core are both characterized as best effort, they are both subject to various types of management to ensure their efficient and reliable operation. Apart from this, application and service providers on the Internet actively monitor and manage their web servers, application stores and other resources. Nonetheless, the degree of management and guarantees for managed services is typically higher than that for the best-effort public Internet. The co-existence of (services and applications) over the public Internet and managed services leads to emergence of the so-called two-lane model [1]. In the two-lane model, the broadband access connection of an end user is used to provide him both with the Internet Access Service and a number of managed services.

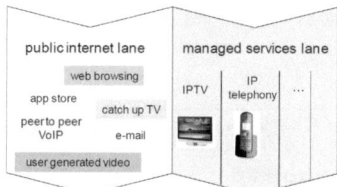

Figure 1: Two Lane model over a single broadband access

In the public Internet lane, the ISP provides an Internet Access Service to the end user. Through this access service, the user gains access to the information and applications on the public Internet. Thus, the user has access to a very large variety of information and applications on the Internet, while he only buys the Internet Access Service from his ISP. In a number of cases, the end user is likely to enter into an agreement or contract with a content provider on the public Internet. These agreements do not involve the ISP and also do not require any action from the ISP. In the managed services lane, the ISP has an agreement with the end user to provide him specific services. There can be a single agreement, made directly between the ISP and the end user. There can also be multiple, interrelated agreements, e.g. one agreement between the end user and a content provider, in combination with a second, related agreement between the content provider and the ISP. Each specific service that an end user buys in the managed services lane requires, in principle, an action by the ISP. Typically, part of this action consists of taking measures to guarantee the quality of the service, for example through the reservation of dedicated bandwidth. In the public Internet lane, no measures are taken to guarantee the quality of specific services.

	Public Internet Lane	Managed services Lane
Services provided by ISP	Single service: access to the global public Internet	Specific service, e.g, IPTV, IP, telephony, etc.
Services provided by other providers	All services on the public Internet ("Over the top services")	Specific services, subject to agreement between other provider and ISP
Agreements between ISP and end user	Single agreement covering Internet access service.	Individual agreements per service
Quality	Best effort (good but no guarantees)	Typically with statistically guaranteed quality for each service.

Table 1: Characteristics of the public Internet lane and the managed services lane

Table 1 summarizes the characteristics of the public Internet lane and the managed services lane. It is seen that there are substantial differences between the two lanes in two areas that are crucial to net neutrality discussion: openness and quality guarantees.

- *Public Internet lane offers more openness.* As discussed earlier, an end user can access all information and buy services from all content providers on the global public Internet via a single Internet access service. In addition to this openness from the end user perspective, there is also openness from the content provider perspective: a content provider connected to the public Internet can reach and provide services to all end users on the global public Internet. The openness in the public Internet lane is obtained through a combination of access and interconnection. The managed service lane, in contrast, has a limited openness. Typically, an end user can only choose among the managed services offered by his own ISP. Also, from the content provider perspective, the openness can be limited: the content provider is heavily dependent on the end user's ISP to provide the service to a particular end user over the managed services lane.

- *The managed services lane offers more quality guarantees.* In the managed services lane, ISPs can, for example, guarantee the availability of bandwidth for specific services or guarantee a small delay of the IP packets. In the public Internet lane, ISPs cannot in general guarantee the quality for specific services, because they handle all traffic using the same best-effort approach. They typically aim to achieve a good quality for the total of the best-effort traffic they transport, within the technical and economic constraints they have, but the performance cannot be guaranteed.

Openness in the public Internet lane

One of the attractive and much valued properties of the public Internet lane is its openness. This section analyses the combination of access and interconnection through which this openness is achieved.

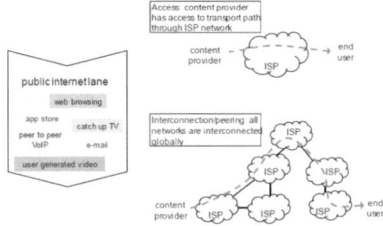

Figure 2: The role of access and interconnection in the public Internet lane

- Through the availability of access at the IP layer (see Figure 2, top right), a content provider can benefit from the IP routing and transport capabilities of the ISP. In essence, the access provides the content provider with a path or connection to the end user he wants to reach. With the access to one ISP network, a content provider can reach all customers of the particular ISP that he is connected to himself.

- Because ISP networks are all typically directly or indirectly interconnected through IP peering and IP transit agreements, a content provider can not only reach end users connected to his own ISP's network, but also end users connected to other ISP networks (Figure 2 bottom right). Because of the extensive interconnection of today's ISP networks, a content provider can in principle reach every end user over the global public Internet.

Thus, the current degree of openness in the public Internet lane requires both access and interconnection. With access only, a content provider can reach only a limited group of end users. If the content provider's end users are distributed over multiple ISP networks, which is a typical situation, it would need to connect its service and application platforms to each of these networks, which is difficult and expensive in practice. It is only with interconnection of networks that a large group of customers can be reached, without the need to know the specific IP connectivity arrangements of individual end users.

Quality guarantees in the managed services lane

An attractive feature of the managed services lane is the ability to guarantee the quality of the service and applications that are delivered. Since the ISP has detailed knowledge of the services that it has agreed to deliver to the end users, it can apply traffic management measures tailored to the specific services involved. This is typically done by combining the IP QoS mechanisms with bandwidth reservations at the layers below the IP layer. The technology to provide QoS assurance on an end to end basis through the entire Internet has been reasonably implementable for perhaps a dozen years, yet there is hardly any actual implementation *between* ISPs, even though QoS is commonly implemented within an ISP. There are technical challenges, to be sure, notably including a lack of standardization of QoS levels;[10] however, the absence of QoS aware interconnection has much more to do with economic and business factors than with technical ones.[8] Among the practical challenges are:

- Limited demonstrated consumer willingness to pay for QoS, presumably because performance in the absence of guarantees is nonetheless sufficient for most purposes.

- Network effects and the initial adoption hump: QoS-aware interconnection has little value until and unless critical masses of ISPs implement it.

- Challenges in verifying that the other network has in fact delivered the service that it has committed: This difficulty is compounded by the understandable reluctance of network operators to make the internal performance of their networks visible to their competitors.

- Challenges with the business model: A basic model for assessing different wholesale charges based on (1) the volume of traffic in conjunction with (2) the class of service requested and delivered has been fairly clear for some time[5]. Actual implementation would have to address not only the measurement issues noted previously, but also possible financial penalties for failing to meet performance level commitments (Service Level Agreements).

If bandwidth reservations in the access network are used to obtain quality guarantees in the managed services layer, then this can also affect the quality of the services delivered through the public Internet lane. Since both lanes are typically provided over a single broadband access connection, they share the network capacity in this part of the transport chain. As a result, bandwidth reservations that are beneficial for service delivery in the managed services lane can lead to a lower quality for services delivered through the public Internet lane.

III Future business models combining quality guarantees and openness

There is, of course, no certainty as to how business models will evolve in the future. In order to clarify possible directions for future evolution, and their relative impact on consumers, we have attempted to identify a number of possible outcomes or scenarios, each based on considerations of a two lane (or multiple lane) Internet. They differ chiefly among three dimensions:

- The quality and bandwidth available to the public lane, in comparison to that available to the managed services lane. Will the public lane offer sufficient bandwidth for over-the-top (OTT) providers? How is the relative balance of bandwidth likely to evolve over time?
- What new services and applications are likely to emerge that might function better with better-then-best-efforts quality? Might the evolution of other sectors (health, energy, transport) drive such applications?
- What market players will have access to the best-efforts lane, and to the managed services lane?

Possible scenarios for the future evolution of the sector include:

- **Little change from today:** A two lane Internet has been technically feasible for at least ten years. That it has appeared to only a very limited extent may mean that consumers do not want it, or at least that commercial incentives are not strong enough to drive the evolution. This is a rather likely option. The managed services lane already exists, but it is used mainly for the TV and telephony components of triple play. These two components compete to only a limited degree with services delivered over the public Internet lane.
- **Continuation and further expansion of two-lane model:** If traffic over the managed services lane were to substantially increase, either due to new applications or due to increased use of the managed services lane for forms of video that today are in the public lane, might they tend to crowd out services in the public Internet lane? This scenario assumes that access remedies remain relative to traditional service, but that the managed services lane is used exclusively by the facilities based ISP for its own "walled garden" of services.
- **ISPs open up the managed services lane to other providers:** In this scenario, not only does the managed services lane expand, but it is made available to competitors of the facilities-based network operators. Capacity planning potentially becomes more complex than it is today.
- **End-to-end service guarantees become possible in the public Internet**: QoS aware interconnection has been technically feasible for many years, but is hardly ever implemented. If it were possible to surmount the quite substantial practical obstacles, new uses of the Internet might be enabled.

In the remainder of this section, we assess these four scenarios in terms of their relative likelihood, and in terms of their implications for competition, innovation, freedom of expression, consumer awareness, and privacy.

Relative likelihood

Given the relative slow pace of change over the past ten to fifteen years in regard to implementation of QoS, it would seem that the most likely scenario reflects only gradual change to the status quo. On the other hand, increasing traffic volumes might drive a more rapid evolution. As part of Cisco Systems' annual review of likely trends in Internet traffic (based largely on a review of likely take-up of VoIP, video, and sectoral applications), they project a gradual but substantial increase in the scope of the managed services lane for both consumer and business traffic [2]. I find their projections plausible.

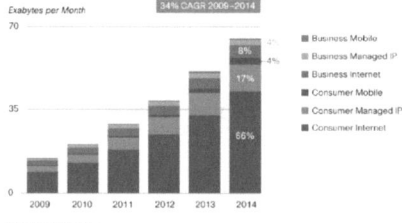

Figure 3: Cisco VNI global overall Internet traffic forecast

This would seem to suggest a steady growth in the importance of the managed services lane, but not necessarily to the point of crowding out services based on the public lane – at least, not for quite some time. We would also caution against simply extrapolating the growth in managed services beyond the period that they have projected – often, there are natural limits to the growth of new services, resulting in S-shaped growth curves that "top out" rather than growing exponentially without limit. The idea that ISPs might open their managed service lane to competitors is perhaps not as far-fetched as it might seem at first blush, even though we are aware of no instance of commercial application today. Several NRAs have considered imposing QoS constraints, with different price levels for different mixes of average delay, jitter, and packet loss. One of our interviewees also indicated that they have a QoS-aware wholesale offer, but no actual take-up. End-to-end guarantees and QoS-aware interconnection pose perhaps the greatest challenges. It is notoriously difficult to bring services over the initial adoption hump in a case like this, which is characterized by strong network effects, long value chains, and high transaction costs (many ISPs that have to somehow find agreement)[7]. For either the "opening the managed services lane" of the "end-to-end guarantees" scenarios, it would be important to arrive at agreed standards on how to interpret QoS. Promising work has been done in this area,[10] but much remains to be done.

Competition

In terms of competition, "little or no change" is familiar and would appear to be acceptable. Further expansion of a two-lane model as a series of broadband ISP-specific "walled gardens" would seem to be a somewhat less attractive model, to the extent that it implies that the broadband ISP's own services become increasingly important, and that third parties might not be able to offer competitive alternatives that depend on special QoS capabilities. This would effectively confer a certain degree of market power on the broadband ISP, even in cases where competitors using LLU, shared access and/or bit stream access were effective. This is already the case today, but it might take on increasing significance if QoS-sensitive applications were to gain in importance. This form of market power would appear likely to enhance the ability of a facilities-based ISP to extract payments from the other side of the market, to the extent that there are applications that depend on better-than-best-efforts service.

This is arguably a negative consequence. There might also be some risk in that scenario of the broadband ISP choosing to permit the public Internet lane to be crowded out in order to make its own manages services lane more attractive in comparison to the offers of competitors; however, NRAs in the EU seem to have adequate tools to deal with this in the form of the minimum QoS authority provided by the 2009 amendments to the regulatory framework. If facilities-based operators were to open their QoS-aware managed service lane to third parties, and if the opening (and other elements of existing regulation) were effective, then one could expect competition to be in good shape. The effect that QoS-aware interconnection would have on competition is heavily dependent on how it is implemented, and by which market players.

Innovation

Innovation is not just a matter of physical network access. In the complicated and potentially multi-sided market of the Internet, gateways of bottlenecks could serve to inhibit the creation of applications. For example, it is impossible to determine which applications might have been developed, but were not, due to the lack of QoS guarantees in the Internet. It is also possible for the *threat* of gate keeping activity to inhibit innovation. From the perspective of innovation, scenarios where there is no gatekeeper will tend to preferable to those where there are bottlenecks, other things being equal. Some have argued that, in the absence of additional payments from content providers to broadband ISPs, the latter will not be motivated to build or maintain their networks. We find this argument unpersuasive; however, from a two-sided market perspective, such payments are not necessarily objectionable. In general, differentiation can help bring to market new goods and services whose QoS requirements exceed or differ from the market's least common denominator.

Freedom of expression

The scenarios that entail a gatekeeper will also tend to be less attractive from the perspective of maintaining freedom of expression; however, National policymakers are unlikely to tolerate limits to freedom of expression, and will find tools to deal with it should problems arise. Examples of network neutrality deviations as a means of interference with freedom of expression have been rare in any case. As a possible example, consider the case of a large US broadband provider that was alleged in 2004 to have systematically filtered all email messages to its subscribers whose content contained the URL of a coalition of activists who opposed the war in Iraq [6].

Consumer awareness

In the communications transparent communication of QoS parameters and network management practices has been a recurrent theme. We think that there may be scope for continued technical and policy research on better (more meaningful, more easily grasped, more repeatable) Internet performance metrics. This is independent of scenario that the sector ultimately follows. The scenarios that entail end-to-end QoS assurance, or where the managed lane becomes available to competitors, might be slightly superior from this perspective. They tend to depend on a degree of standardization of QoS, which is likely to be more readily grasped by consumers.

Privacy

The intersection between network neutrality and privacy is rather limited. The primary concern is that managed services could be implemented by means of Deep Packet Inspection, and that DPI potentially makes a great deal of individual data available to the ISP. The key questions still relate to how the data is used, and how and for how long it is retained. These are still addressed by the e-Privacy Directive. Given that DPI can be used in any of the scenarios (including the "little or no change" scenario), this is not a reason to prefer one scenario over another.

Comparative assessment

Table 2 provides a rough assessment of the relative merits of the alternative evolutionary scenarios. As with any table of this type, it should be interpreted with some care. QoS-aware interconnection is in some ways the most promising of the scenarios, but it is also the least likely to emerge.

	Little or no change	Increasing significance of the two-lane model	Open up managed services lane to other providers	QoS-aware inter-connection in the public Internet
Competition	0	-	+	?
Innovation	0	-	+	++
Freedom of expression	0	-	0	0
Consumer awareness	0	0	+	++
Privacy	0	0	0	0

0 = no change; + = better; ++ = still better; - = worse; -- = still worse

Table 2: Relative merits of different Internet evolutionary scenarios.

IV Evidence-based net neutrality regulation

The Internet's evolution is dynamic and complex. The availability and design of a suitable regulatory response must reflect this dynamism, and also the responsiveness of regulators and market players to each other. Therefore, national legislation should be future proof and avoid being overly prescriptive, to avoid a premature response to the emerging environment. Regulators expecting a 'smoking gun' to present itself should be advised against such a reactive approach. A more proactive approach to monitoring and researching non-neutral behaviors will make network operators much more cognizant of their duties and obligations. The pace of change in the relation between architecture and content on the Internet requires continuous improvement in the regulator's research and technological training. This is in part a reflection of the complexity of the issue set, including security and Internet peering issues, as well as more traditional telecoms and content issues. Regulators can monitor both commercial transactions and traffic shaping by ISPs to detect potentially abusive discrimination. No matter what theoretical powers may exist, their usage in practice and the issue of forensic gathering of evidence may ultimately be more important. An ex ante requirement to demonstrate internal network metrics to content provider customers and consumers may be a practical solution. Should packet discrimination be introduced, the types of harmful discrimination that can result may be undetectable by consumers and regulators. Blocking is relatively easy to spot, but 'throttling' or choking bandwidth may be more difficult. A solution may be to require network operators to provide their Service Level Agreements both to content providers and more transparently to the end-user via a regulatory or co-regulatory reporting requirement. Strong arguments remain for ensuring that ISPs inform consumers when they reach a monthly download limit or 'cap', ensuring no return to the rationed per-minute or per-byte Internet use. As the law and practice stand today, it seems that most customers do not know when they have been targeted as over-strenuous users of the Internet, only that their connection has slowed. Once targeted, customers generally cannot prove their 'innocence' – they have to accept the Terms of Use of the ISP without appeal (except theoretically via courts for breach of contract, or regulator for infringement of their consumer rights). The number of alternative ISPs is shrinking – not only is the ISP business expensive, leading to concentration in the industry, but the costs of renting backhaul from dominant operators is sufficiently high that no ISP would want to offer service to a suspected 'bandwidth hog'. We may expect to see more protest behavior by 'netizens' who do not agree with these policies, especially where ISPs are seen to have failed to inform end-users fully about the implications of policy changes. Regulators and politicians are challenged publicly by such problems, particularly given the ubiquity of email, Twitter and social media protests against censorship. Regulators will need to ensure that the network operators report more fully and publicly the levels of connectivity that they provide between themselves as well as

to end-users. Internet architecture experts have explained that discrimination is most likely to occur at this level as it is close to undetectable by those not in the two networks concerned in the handover of content. A reporting requirement will need to be imposed if voluntary agreement is not possible. As this information is routinely collected by the network operators for internal purposes, it should not impose a substantial burden. Regulators should be wary of imposing costs on ISPs that are disproportionate. Very high entry barrier co-regulation and self-regulation can curb market entry. Onerous regulation (including self-regulation) leads towards closed and concentrated structures, for three reasons:
1. Larger companies are better able to bear compliance costs;
2. Larger companies have the lobbying power to seek to influence regulation;
3. Dominant and entrenched market actors in regulated 'bottlenecks' play games with regulators in order to increase the sunk costs of market entry for other actors, and can pass through costs to consumers and innovators in non-competitive markets.
Therefore any solution needs to take note of the potential for larger companies to 'game' a co-regulatory scheme and create additional compliance costs for smaller companies (whether content or network operators and the combination of sectors makes this a particularly complex regulatory 'game'). The need for greater research towards understanding the nature of congestion problems on the Internet and their effect on content and innovation is clear [9][11].

Conclusions:
There have been scattered complaints, some of them credible, of (1) mobile network operators (MNOs) blocking or charging excessive prices for VoIP, and of (2) blocking or throttling of traffic such as file sharing. Despite all of this, possible concerns for the future remain.This are a policy area with no perfect solutions. Of course the Internet should be open to all, but private investment is the critical component in building a faster Internet. Of course universal service should be supported, and there must be some minimum access to the open Internet for all, whether they use a mobile 3G connection or a fast IPTV-enabled premium service. In light of the current state of play, we think that it is important to avoid inappropriate, disproportionate, or premature action. Based on the findings noted in the previous section, our key recommendations are:
· Do not impose any further network neutrality obligations until there is sufficient experience with the obligations already imposed through the 2009 amendments to the regulatory framework to make a reasoned judgment about their effectiveness;
· Support both technical and policy research to enhance the effectiveness of the consumer transparency obligations, and to ensure that the minimum QoS obligations can be effectively imposed should they prove to be needed;
· Continue to study the aspects of network neutrality where complaints may have some basis, including (1) charges and conditions that mobile operators impose on providers of Voice over IP (VoIP), and (2) impairment of peer-to-peer traffic.
I am happier limiting my conclusions to emphasize the complexity of the problem than trying to claim a one-sizefits-all solution.

REFERENCES

[1] BEREC (Body of European Regulators for Electronic Communications): Response to the European commission's consultation on the open Internet and net neutrality in Europe, BoR (10) 42, 30 September 2010,
http://www.erg.eu.int/doc/berec/bor_10_42.pdf.

[2] Cisco VNI: Hyper connectivity and the Approaching Zetta byte Era, 2 June 2010.

[3] FCC (Federal Communications Commission): In the Matter of Preserving the Open Internet, Broadband Industry Practices, GN Docket No. 09-191, WC Docket No. 07-52, October 22, 2009,
http://hraunfoss.fcc.gov/edocs_public/attachmatch/FCC-09-93A1.doc.

[4] FCC (Federal Communications Commission): In the Matter of Preserving the Open Internet; Broadband Industry Practices; GN Docket No. 09-191, WC Docket No. 07-52, 23 December 2010.

[5] Laffont, J.-J., Marcus, J. S., Rey, P. and J. Tirole, IDE-I, Toulouse: Internet interconnection and the off-net-cost pricing principle, RAND Journal of Economics, Vol. 34, No. 2, Summer 2003, available at
http://www.rje.org/abstracts/abstracts/2003/rje.sum03.Laffont.pdf.

[6] Marcus et al.: Network Neutrality: Implications for Europe, WIK, January 2009.

[7] Marcus, J. S.: Evolving Core Capabilities of the Internet, Journal on Telecommunications and High Technology Law, 2004, available at:
http://papers.ssrn.com/sol3/papers.cfm?abstract_id=921903.

[8] Marcus, J. S.: Framework for Interconnection of IP-Based Networks – Accounting Systems and Interconnection Regimes in the USA and the UK, 27 March 2006, available at:
http://www.bundesnetzagentur.de/media/archive/6201.pdf.

[9] Marsden, C., Simmons, S., Brown, I., Woods, L., Peake, A., Robinson, N. et al. (2008) 'Options for and Effectiveness of Internet Selfand Co-regulation Phase 2: Case Study Report', 15 January. Prepared for European Commission DG Information Society & Media. Available from: http://ssrn.com/abstract=1281374

[10] MIT QoS WG: Inter-provider Quality of Service, White paper draft 1.1, 17 November 2006, available at:
http://cfp.mit.edu/publications/CFP_Papers/Interprovider%20QoS%20MIT_CFP_WP_9_14_06.pdf.

[11] Zittrain, J. (2008) The Future of the Internet and How to Stop It. New Haven, CT: Yale University Press.